A Special Gift

For:

_____

From:

_____

Date:

_____

Copyright © 1995
Brownlow Publishing Company
6309 Airport Freeway
Fort Worth, Texas 76117

ISBN: 1-57051-045-8

Cover/Interior:
Koechel Peterson & Associates

Printed in Singapore

Faithful Friends

Brownlow

Brownlow Publishing Company, Inc.

Little Treasures
Miniature Books

A Little Cup of Tea

All Things Great & Small

Angels of Friendship

Baby's First Little Bible

Baby's First Book of Angels

Cherished Bible Stories

Dear Teacher

Faith

Faithful Friends

Flowers of Graduation

For My Secret Pal

From Friend to Friend

Grandmothers Are for Loving

Hope

Love

Mother

My Sister, My Friend

Precious Are the Promises

Quilted Hearts

Soft as the Voice of an Angel

The Night the Angels Sang

A Quiet Friendship

The very best thing is good talk, and the thing that helps it most is friendship. How it dissolves the barriers that divide us, and loosens all constraints, and diffuses itself through all the veins of life— this feeling that we understand and trust each other, and wish each other heartily well!

Everything into which it really comes is good. It transforms letter writing from a task to a pleasure. It makes music a thousand times more sweet. Yes, there is a talkability that can express itself even without words. There is an exchange of thoughts and feeling which is happily alike in speech and in silence. It is quietness pervaded with friendship.

HENRY VAN DYKE

Something like home
that is not home
is to be desired,
it is found in
the house of a friend.

SIR W. TEMPLE

Peace cannot be
kept by force.
It can only be achieved
by understanding.

ALBERT EINSTEIN

The Beauty of Peace

Drop thy still dews of quietness,

Till all our strivings cease;

Take from our souls

the strain and stress,

And let our ordered lives confess

The beauty of thy peace.

JOHN GREENLEAF WHITTIER

Friendships do not grow up in any carefully tended and contemplated fashion.... They begin haphazard.

As we look back on the first time we saw our friends we find that generally our original impression was curiously astray. We have worked along beside them, have grown to cherish their delicious absurdities, have outrageously imposed on each other's patience—and suddenly we awoke to realize what had happened.

We had, without knowing it, gained a new friend.

CHRISTOPHER MORLEY

I am not bound
to make the world go right,
But only to discover
and to do,
With cheerful heart,
the work that
God appoints.

JEAN INGELOW

Solitude

It is in solitude that we discover that being is more important than having, and that we are worth more than the result of our efforts. In solitude we discover that our life is not a possession to be defended, but a gift to be shared. It's there we recognize

that the healing words we
speak are not just our own,
but are given to us; that the
love we can express is part of a
greater love; and that the new
life we bring forth is not a
property to cling to, but a gift
to be received.

HENRI J. M. NOUWEN

*Each moment of the year
has its own beauty...
a picture which was never
seen before and which shall
never be seen again.*

RALPH WALDO EMERSON

*Where there is great love
there are always miracles.*

WILLA CATHER

*If I had known
what trouble you were bearing;
What griefs were in
the silence of your face;
I would have been
more gentle and more caring,
And tried to give you
gladness for a space.*

MARY CAROLYN DAVIES

Peace does not dwell in outward things, but within the soul; we may preserve it in the midst of the bitterest pain if our will remain firm and submissive. Peace in this life springs from acquiescence, not in an exemption from suffering.

FRANÇOIS FÉNELON

Let friend
trust friend,
and love demand
love's like.

ROBERT BROWNING

At Home

God's thoughts, his will,
his love, his judgments
are all man's home. To think
his thoughts, to choose his
will, to love his loves, to judge
his judgments, and thus to
know that he is in us, is to be
at home.

GEORGE MACDONALD

Harmonious Living

Unite contemplation with action. They are not contradictory and incompatible, but mutually helpful to each other. Contemplation will strengthen for action, and action sends us back to contemplation, and thus the inner and outer life will be harmoniously developed.

SAMUEL FOOTE

The ideal of

friendship

is to

feel as one,

while

remaining

two.

MADAME SWETCHINE

Talk not of wasted affection,
affection was never wasted.
If it enrich not the heart of another,
its waters, returning
Back to their springs, like the rain,
shall fill them
full of refreshment.
That which the fountain sends forth
returns again to the fountain.
Patience; accomplish thy labour,
accomplish thy work of affection.

HENRY WADSWORTH LONGFELLOW

The friendship between
me and you I will not
compare to a chain;
for that the rains might rust,
or the falling tree might break.

BANCROFT

One of the most beautiful
qualities of true friendship
is to understand
and to be understood.

SENECA

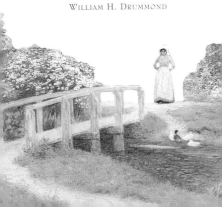

*What sweet delight
a quiet life affords.*

WILLIAM H. DRUMMOND

He who does not
understand your silence
will probably not understand
your words.

ELBERT GREEN HUBBARD

Happiness quite unshared
can scarcely be
called happiness;
it has no taste.

CHARLOTTE BRONTË

Heart and Home

May joy in full measure
Rain down on your way,
May all that gives pleasure
Surround you today:
Beyond all expressing
May years yet to come
Be laden with blessing
For heart and for home.

H. M. B.

Like Honey in a Jar

I admire people who are suited to the contemplative life, but I am not one of them. They can sit inside themselves like honey in a jar and just be. It's wonderful to have someone like that around, you always feel you can count on them. You

can go away and come back,
you can change your mind and
your hairdo and your politics,
and when you get through
doing all these upsetting
things, you look around and
there they are, just the way they
were, just being.

ELIZABETH JANEWAY

All the

troubles of life

come upon us

because we refuse

to sit quietly

for a while each day

in our room.

BLAISE PASCAL

*To know one's self
is the true;
To strive with one's self
is the good;
To conquer one's self
is the beautiful.*

JOSEPH ROUX

Conversation
enriches the
understanding,
but solitude
is the school
of genius.

EDWARD GIBBON

True contentment is a real,
even an active, virtue—not
only affirmative but creative.
It is the power of getting
out of any situation
all there is in it.

G. K. CHESTERTON

Peace is the
deliberate adjustment of
my life to the will of God.

A Half Hour

An old Danish peasant
on his deathbed
asked of his son
only one promise:
that he should sit alone
for a half-hour each day
in the best room in the house.
The son did this and
became a model citizen
for the whole district.

Dedicate some of
your life to others.
Your dedication
will not be a sacrifice;
It will be an
exhilarating experience.

THOMAS DOOLEY

*Quiet minds cannot
be perplexed or frightened,
but go on in fortune or misfortune
at their own private pace,
like a clock in a thunderstorm.*

ROBERT LOUIS STEVENSON

*Lose no chance
of giving pleasure.*

FRANCES R. HAVERGAL

Love may strive,
but vain is the endeavor
All its boundless riches to unfold;
Still its tenderest, truest secrets linger
Ever in the deepest depth untold.

ADELAIDE A. PROCTER

*When people
are serving,
life is no longer
meaningless.*

JOHN W. GARDNER

*Dear friends,
since God so loved us,
we also ought to
love one another.*

1 JOHN 4:11

May the

hinges

of friendship

never rust,

Nor the

wings of love

lose a feather.

EDWARD BANNERMAN
RAMSEY

*No man has a right
to lead such a life of
contemplation as to forget
in his own ease
the service due to his neighbor;
nor has any man a right
to be so immersed in active life
as to neglect the
contemplation of God.*

AUGUSTINE

Traveling in the company

of those we love

is home in motion.

LEIGH HUNT

Contentment consists

not in great wealth

but in few wants.

EPICTETUS

Without love and kindness, life is cold, selfish, and uninteresting, and leads to distaste for everything. With kindness, the difficult becomes easy, the obscure clear; life assumes a charm and its miseries are softened. If we knew the power of kindness, we should transform this world into a paradise.

CHARLES WAGNER

All the Best

There are some men and women in whose company we are always at our best. All the best stops in our nature are drawn out, and we find a music in our souls never felt before.

HENRY DRUMMOND

There is a loftier ambition
than merely to stand
high in the world.
It is to stoop down
and lift mankind
a little higher.

HENRY VAN DYKE

My fellow,

my companion,

held most dear,

My soul,

my other self,

my inward friend.

MARY SIDNEY HERBERT

We meet on the broad pathway of good faith and good will; no advantage shall be taken on either side, but all shall be openness and love.

WILLIAM PENN

A Beloved Friend

A beloved friend does not fill one part of the soul, but, penetrating the whole, becomes connected with all feeling.

A friend is he who sets his heart upon us, is happy with us, and delights in us; does for us what we want, is willing and fully engaged to do all he can for us, on whom we can rely in all cases.

A true friend embraces our objects as his own. We feel another mind bent on the same end, enjoying it, ensuring it, reflecting it, and delighting in our devotion to it.

Other blessings may be taken away, but if we have acquired a good friend by goodness, we have a blessing which improves in value when others fail. It is even heightened by sufferings.

To be only an admirer is not to be a friend of a human being. Human nature wants something more, and our perceptions are diseased when we dress up a human being in the attributes of divinity. He is our friend who loves more than admires us, and would aid us in our great work.

WILLIAM ELLERY CHANNING

*He who
sees a need
and waits
to be asked
for help
is as unkind
as if he had
refused it.*

DANTE ALIGHIERI

Everything
true and great
grows in silence.
Without silence
we fall short
of reality
and cannot
plumb the depths
of being.

LADISLAUS BOROS

Recipe for Happiness

Combine 4 parts of Contentment,
2 parts of Joy
and 1 part Pleasure.
But these ingredients
must be grown
in one's own garden.
Sometimes they may be
obtained of a Good Friend.
When so procured, a fair return
must be made else Happiness
spoils and becomes trouble.

*Sometimes Discontent
and Ambition
have been combined in a
desire to obtain Happiness
but Fame and Wealth
have resulted and persons
who have tasted these say
they are inferior substitutes.*

UNKNOWN

I want to live by the side of the road and be a friend to man.

SAM WALTER FOSS

Of all the ways of awakening inner reverence in man, the best is the contemplation of the works of God. Their transcendent greatness must inspire awe.

ELIJAH DE VIDAS

He that wrongs his friend
Wrongs himself more,
and ever bears about
A silent court of justice
in his breast,
Himself the judge and jury,
and himself
The prisoner at the bar
ever condemned.

ALFRED, LORD TENNYSON

Those Who Listen

Listening is a magnetic and strange thing, a creative force. The friends who listen to us are the ones we move toward, and we want to sit in their radius. When we are listened to, it creates us, makes us unfold and expand.

KARL AUGUSTUS MENNINGER

Friendship
is infinitely
better than
kindness.

CICERO

Nothing will make us

so charitable and tender

to the faults of others as,

by self-examination,

thoroughly to know our own.

FRANÇOIS FÉNELON

Friends, books,

a cheerful heart

and conscience clear

Are the most

choice companions

we have here.

WILLIAM MATHER

*The mouth keeps silent
to hear the heart speak.*

ALFRED DE MUSSET

The World Within

Glorious indeed is the

world of God around us,

but more glorious the

world of God within us.

There lies the land of song;

there lies the poet's native land.

HENRY WADSWORTH LONGFELLOW

The Gift of Serenity

*Practice the art of aloneness
and you will discover
the treasure of tranquility.
Develop the art of
solitude and you will
unearth the gift of serenity.*

WILLIAM ARTHUR WARD

We have been
friends together
in sunshine
and in shade.

CAROLINE NORTON

Contentment

*Nine requisites
for contented living:*

• *Health enough to make
work a pleasure;*

• *Wealth enough to
support your needs;*

• *Strength to battle
with difficulties
and overcome them;*

• *Grace enough to confess
your sins and forsake them;*

• *Patience enough to toil until some good is accomplished;*

• *Charity enough to see some good in your neighbor;*

• *Love enough to move you to be useful and helpful to others;*

• *Faith enough to make real the things of God;*

• *Hope enough to remove all anxious fears concerning the future.*

JOHANN WOLFGANG VON GOETHE

Language has created
the word loneliness *to express*
the pain of being alone, and
the word solitude *to express*
the glory of being alone.

PAUL TILLICH

The greatest ideas,
the most
profound thoughts,
and the most
beautiful poetry
are born from
the womb of silence.

WILLIAM ARTHUR WARD

Sweet Flower

Sweet Flower—that speaks
of friendship true
Will bring my
special wish to you,
May health and
happiness be near
To bless each day
throughout the year.

NINETEENTH-CENTURY
GREETING CARD

*To know someone
here or there
with whom you can
feel there is understanding
in spite of distances or
thoughts unexpressed—
that can make
this life a garden.*

JOHANN WOLFGANG VON GOETHE

The capacity to
care gives life
its deepest
significance.

PABLO CASALS

Be still
and know
that I
am God.

PSALM 46:10

Where We Belong

Joy of life seems to me to arise from a sense of being where one belongs.... All the discontented people I know are trying sedulously to be something they are not, to do something they cannot do. Contentment, and indeed usefulness, comes as the infallible result of great acceptances, great humilities—of not trying to make ourselves this or that (to conform to some dramatized version of ourselves), but of surrendering ourselves to the fullness of life—of letting life flow through us.

DAVID GRAYSON

We are born helpless.
As soon as we are fully
conscious we discover loneliness.
We need others physically,
emotionally, intellectually;
we need them if we are
to know anything,
even ourselves.

C. S. LEWIS

Go oft to the house
of thy friend,
for weeds choke
the unused path.

RALPH WALDO EMERSON

The good
and the wise
lead quiet lives.

EURIPIDES

Thou, Friendship!—Thou,

my grief beguilest,

Thy hand heals

many a rankling wound,

Life's wounds are lightened

when thou smilest,

Thee have I sought,

and thee have found!

SCHILLER